A HELPING
HAND

WHAT ABOUT NEKO?

Quarto is the authority on a wide range of topics.
Quarto educates, entertains and enriches the lives of
our readers—enthusiasts and lovers of hands-on living.
www.quartoknows.com

Author: Nancy Loewen
Illustrator: Elisa Paganelli
Editors: Ellie Brough and Vicky Garrard
Designer: Victoria Kimonidou
Consultant: Joanna Silver

© 2020 Quarto Publishing plc

This edition first published in 2020 by QED Publishing,
an imprint of The Quarto Group.
The Old Brewery, 6 Blundell Street,
London N7 9BH, United Kingdom.
T (0)20 7700 6700 F (0)20 7700 8066
www.QuartoKnows.com

A catalogue record for this book is available from the British Library.

ISBN 978 0 7112 5101 4

9 8 7 6 5 4 3 2 1

Manufactured in Guangdong, China TT032020

MIX
Paper from
responsible sources
FSC® C016973
FSC
www.fsc.org

All web addresses included at the back of this
book were correct at the time of printing.
The publisher cannot be held responsible for the
content of the websites referred to in this book.

WHAT ABOUT NEKO?

A story about divorce

BY
NANCY LOEWEN

ART BY
ELISA PAGANELLI

Becca woke up the same way she did every day –
with her face covered in dog kisses!

"All right, Neko," she said,
giggling. "Let's go on our
walk with Daddy."

Then she remembered.
Daddy didn't live with them anymore.

In the kitchen, Becca's big brother,
David, was arguing with Mum.

"David, this is not a choice," Mum told him.
"Every morning you need to walk Neko, just
like Daddy used to. Becca can go with you."

"But I don't –"

"No buts," Mum said. "Now go."

On their walk, Neko's tail wagged the same as ever.

She sniffed Mr Moe's garden gnome and licked up Mrs Ellery's spilt birdseed, like always.

But Becca felt sure that Neko was just pretending. "Do you think Neko misses Daddy?" Becca asked David.

"Probably," David said.

"I think Daddy misses Neko, too," Becca said. "A lot."

At breakfast, Mum reminded them that Daddy would be picking them up after school. It was Friday – time for their Daddy weekend.

"Can we take Neko with us this time?" Becca begged. "Please?"

"You know Daddy can't have dogs in his flat," Mum said.

"That's a stupid rule!" Becca said. She ran to her room.

Becca threw herself on her bed. There were
so many things she didn't understand.

Like why Mum and
Daddy couldn't stay
together. She didn't
think she would ever
understand that.

And what about Neko? Neko was a super-smart dog, but the only words she understood were ones like 'sit' and 'good girl'. She didn't understand words like 'divorce' and 'custody'.

Mum came into Becca's room and sat on the floor.

"Mummy... if Daddy doesn't get to see Neko very often, do you think he'll forget her?" Becca asked.

"Oh, honey, no," Mum said.
"Not a chance."

She put her hand on top of Becca's.
"This is hard for all of us," she said.
"But Daddy and I love you and David and
Neko very much. We'll work something out."

After school, Becca and David watched for Daddy's car.
But Mum pulled up instead. Neko was in the car too.

"Is Daddy okay?" Becca asked,
worried. "Aren't we going to
see him today?"

"Everything's fine," Mum said. She was smiling.

"Daddy and I decided there's a much better place for him to pick you up on your Daddy weekends..."

It was the park! And there was Daddy!
Neko bolted out of the car, her tail wagging
wildly. Becca followed close behind.

"Neko!" Daddy exclaimed.
"Who's my good dog?"

As Becca watched Neko jump all over Daddy,
David and Mum stood by the car.

"Go on," Mum said to David. "The three of you can
take Neko for a walk and then I'll take her home."

Daddy looked over at Mum.
"Thank you," he said.

Then Daddy lifted Becca up and spun her around.
"Ugh!" she teased. "Your face smells like dog kisses!"

NEXT STEPS

How can you help your child feel whole during the divorce process?

The ground is unsteady

We all want the best for our children. But life isn't perfect, and sometimes, despite our best efforts, we bring uncertainty, anger or fear into their lives. That may well be the case during a divorce. And while divorce is common, that doesn't make it any easier for your child. All they know is that their family is changing. The ground is unsteady beneath their feet.

Time to talk

You won't be able to shield your child entirely, but you can lessen the negative impact. Most importantly, reassure your child that both parents love them and that the divorce is not their fault. We adults might not understand how a child could blame themselves for a divorce, but it's almost universal that children feel guilt and regret. And don't forget to listen, too. Allow your child the time and space to talk about their feelings. Acknowledge what they say, even if it might be painful for you to hear.

Self-care is important too

As important as it is to put your child first, do make an effort to take care of yourself, too. Seek out the support you need so that when you are with your child, you can be the parent you want to be. Even in the midst of stress and loss, there will be moments of laughter and beauty. Soak them up, and teach your child to do the same.

Look to the future

Over time, the emotions accompanying a divorce will lessen, for all of you. The divorce will become part of your family history – a challenge that you successfully overcame as you headed towards a new life and a bright future.

SIGNS YOUR CHILD MAY BE STRUGGLING

- Reverting to younger behaviours: clinginess, bedwetting and so on
- Extreme mood swings
- Trying to be 'perfect'
- Refusing to spend time with one parent
- Having headaches and stomach aches
- Sleeping problems: insomnia, bad dreams, wanting to sleep with you
- Eating too little or too much
- A drop in school performance
- Defiant behaviour

EXPRESSING FEELINGS

There are many different ways to help your child express their feelings.

Opportunity

First, don't put children on the spot about sharing their feelings. Instead, offer them ample opportunities to talk, and be sensitive to their moods. Often children feel more comfortable talking if they are doing another activity at the same time, such as riding in a car, going for a walk or playing a board game.

Write a letter

Children may be afraid of expressing feelings of anger and blame to their parents. They might find it helpful to write letters to their parents instead. Children don't need to share these letters with you, but if they do want you to read the letters, make sure they know that you will not judge or punish them for what they write.

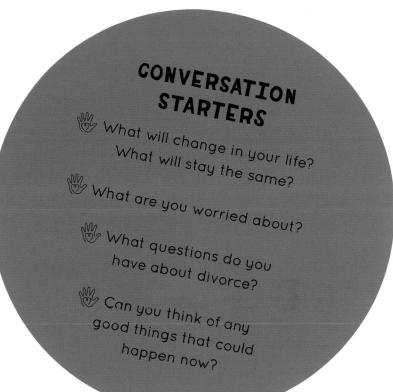

CONVERSATION STARTERS

- What will change in your life? What will stay the same?
- What are you worried about?
- What questions do you have about divorce?
- Can you think of any good things that could happen now?

Keep a diary

Older children may want to keep a diary. Tell them they can write about whatever they want. Keeping a diary could be a helpful activity for the whole family. If children see that writing in a diary helps you, they will be more likely to try it. (Be sure to keep your diary in a private place if you are writing about adult matters.)

Draw

Some children may find drawing easier than talking or writing. Encourage them to explore their hopes and fears through their pictures, and ask them to tell you about what they've drawn.

Role Play

Role-playing games with puppets or other toys can be a good way for children to process their feelings. Follow your child's cues on whether you join in or observe.

HOW TO MAKE THE GROUND STEADY

The transition period can be tough but there are ways you can make it easier.

 ### Routines are key
Following routines can be very helpful in times of stress. Do your best to keep your home life as predictable as possible. If your plans change, discuss it with your child ahead of time.

 ### Present a united front
Ideally, you and your child's other parent should maintain a united front on matters relating to your child's care. That might not always be possible, but it should always be something to strive for.

 ### Always take the high ground
Don't say negative things about the other parent in front of your child. Remember, your child's own identity comes in part from the other parent. Badmouthing the other parent is likely to make your child feel bad, too.

FURTHER RESOURCES

www.gingerbread.org.uk/
A non-profit organisation that provides support and help for single parent families.

www.youngminds.org.uk/find-help/for-parents/ parents-guide-to-support-a-z/parents-guide-to-support-divorce-or-separation/
Advice on supporting your child through the divorce process and after from Young Minds – a mental health non-profit.